How To Buy Your First Home in Minnesota

A Guide To Buying Your First Home in the Twin Cites

All rights are reserved. No part of this book may be reproduced or transmitted in any form or by any means, electronic or mechanical, including photocopying and recording, or by an information storage and retrieval system, without the written consent from the author or co-author.

www.KenGraczak.com

KenGraczak@Gmail.com

Printed in the United States of America

ISBN-13: 978-1519254467

ISBN-10: 1519254466

Co-Written with *"John Maxwell Leadership Coach"* Tim Davis

Copyright © 2015 by Ken Graczak

All rights reserved.

About the Author

After high school in 1994, I moved to the Minneapolis / St. Paul Metro. Over the last 21 years since moving here, I have purchased two homes. The Minneapolis / St. Paul Metro has been a great place to grow up, and has become a great place for my wife Stephanie and I to raise our two children.

I have tried to share the most essential questions that need to be asked and the bigger picture answers. My goal with this book is to settle the fears many new buyers have and eliminate the frustrations that unanswered questions cause. This is especially important for those people that have never been through the home buying process. I was a renter for many years, here and unfortunately that was longer than it really needed to be. In hindsight, I would have been qualified after only a couple years of renting. I was too scared to ask the tough questions. I didn't know where to turn for answers. You can imagine how disappointing it is to look back and add up all the money I wasted renting.

I am thankful everyday that I get to live and work in a community this friendly and vibrant. Whether attending some of our professional sports events (SKOL Vikings) or going to the Minneapolis Sculpture Garden or the St. Paul Children's Museum there always seems to be something family and community based to do here in the Minneapolis / St. Paul Metro.

The Minneapolis / St. Paul Metro is a great place to call home. I anticipate seeing more people purchase a home in the area. I look forward to hearing about YOUR home buying experience.

Read what clients are saying about Ken Graczak…..

As a young first time buyer, I learned a lot about the process. We knew what was going on throughout the process. This was a great experience for my family.

---Kendrick

Kens team was great! He was always available to help us through every step of the mortgage process. He made our dream of homeownership a possibility!

---Alyssa

Ken was very organized and fast at getting us information. He made the process very easy and stress free.

---Alicia

Ken and his staff did a great job working with us to find our home. Their response was very quick and reliable. They were able to help us meet our goals. We will definitely use them again and highly recommend them and their service to anyone!

---Sean

Ken was fantastic. He was prompt, efficient and professional. I will work with him all over again

---Emmanuel T.

I was thrilled by Ken's assistance all the way. His patience was beyond and above normal standard. I acknowledge and reckon Ken's positive attitude even when the situation was at a deadlock. I won't hesitate referring anyone dear to me to you. All in all, I feel lucky and blessed to be a homeowner and I can't thank Ken enough.

---Richard O.

It was the best experience of my life! Ken and his team were professional and met all the needs we needed for our situation. I look forward to my friends and family having the same experience as I did.

---Tawanna W.

My experience with Ken was fantastic. I never had to worry about anything all the entire way through. He let me know what information I needed to get him and when he needed it by. I talked to other people who used other mortgage companies and they had to send in the same documents over and over. Not with Ken's team! Really exceptional service and I recommend him very highly.

---Kathrine R.

I'm very happy with the outcome and professionalism of the people who worked with me in closing my first house. Without the untiring commitment that the people on Ken's Team have shown, it would have been impossible for me to have my new home. Thank you for all your hard work.

---Joel B.

LEGAL NOTICE

The Publisher has strived to be as accurate and complete as possible in the creation of this report, notwithstanding the fact that he does not warrant or represent at any time that the contents within are accurate due to the rapidly changing nature of the market and business.

While all attempts have been made to verify information provided in this publication, the Publisher assumes no responsibility for errors, omissions, or contrary interpretation of the subject matter herein. Any perceived slights of specific persons, peoples, or organizations are unintentional.

In practical advice books, like anything else in life, there are no guarantees of income made. Readers are cautioned to reply on their own judgment about their individual circumstances to act accordingly.

This book is not intended for use as a source of legal, business, accounting or financial advice. All readers are advised to seek services of competent professionals in legal, business, accounting, and finance field.

Introduction	**9**
New Homes vs. Older Homes	*10*
Which Home To Choose?	*11*
Chapter 1 - Location, Location, Location	**13**
Finding The Right Neighborhood	*13*
How Clean Is This Neighborhood?	*14*
Is This A High Crime Area?	*15*
What Is The Average Home Value In The Neighborhood?	*15*
Are There Community Bylaws?	*16*
What Is The Home Close To?	*16*
Is There Garbage Pickup?	*17*
City Life vs. Country Living	*17*
Making The Commute	*20*
Schools In The Area	*21*
Grocery Shopping And Other Necessities	*22*
Other Location Considerations	*23*
Chapter 2 - Working with Real Estate Agent	**25**
Choosing A Real Estate Agent	*25*
Experienced Agents vs. New Agents	*28*
Pushy Agents	*29*
Absentee Agents	*29*
Hard Working Agents	*30*
Preparing To See Homes With Your Agent-Create A List	*31*
Viewing Homes	*32*
Taking Pictures	*32*
Narrowing Down Your Choices	*33*
Information Real Estate Agents Should Tell You	*34*
Working With Sellers And Buyers Agents	*36*
Negotiations With Sellers	*36*
Paperwork	*37*
Survey Neighborhoods	*37*
More Reasons To Hire A Real Estate Agent	*38*
Chapter 3 - Playing the Housing Market: Buying vs. Renting a Home	**40**
Watching The Housing Market	*40*
Making The Most Of The Housing Market	*42*
National Interest Rates For Mortgages	*42*
Building Rates In Your Area	*43*
Number Of Foreclosures In Your Area	*43*
Stock Market And Gasoline Prices	*44*
In The End	*45*

Buying vs. Renting (Pros/Cons)	*45*
Rent To Own	*48*
New Homes	*49*
Using The Housing Market To Your Advantage	*51*

Chapter 4 - Home Inspections — 53

The Importance Of Home Inspections	*53*
How To Find A Home Inspector	*55*
What To Expect From A Home Inspection	*57*
Specific Places That Should Be Inspected	*58*
How Homeowners Will React	*60*
Ways A Home Inspection Can Lower The Final Price	*62*
The Final Walkthrough	*64*
The Closing	*65*
When To Walk Away	*66*

Chapter 5 - Financing Your First Home — 69

Types Of Home Loans	*69*
Where To Find A Lender	*73*
Applying For A Home Loan	*74*
What Not To Do When Applying For A Home Loan	*77*
Increase Your Chances For Approval	*80*
How Home Appraisals Can Affect Your Home Loan	*81*
Additional Fees For Home Loans	*84*
Loan Estimate	*84*
Escrow And Other Loans Terms	*85*

Chapter 6 - Making a Realistic Offer — 89

What To Do Before Making An Offer	*89*
How To Write A Purchase Offer	*91*
Making An Offer	*92*
Low Or High Offers	*93*
Making The Right Offer	*94*
How To Handle A Counter Offer And Offer Rejection	*95*
Considering Items In The Home	*97*
Understanding The Seller	*98*
What To Do In A Buyer's Market	*99*
What To Do In A Seller's Market	*101*

Chapter 7 - Contracts, Home Warranties, and the Closing — 103

Contracts	*103*
Home Warranties	*106*
Closing	*107*

Conclusion — 109

Introduction

If you are currently living in an apartment or renting a house, you may be thinking about buying a home of your own for yourself and your family. This can be an exciting time. Looking at properties, deciding whether to buy a home or build a new one, and finding financing will take up a lot of your time.

There will be a long list of things you will need to do before you buy a home. This list includes:

- Finding the right neighborhood
- Finding a home that is big enough
- Finding the features you are looking for
- Choosing the right size yard
- Choosing a real estate agent
- Understanding the housing market
- The ins and outs of home inspection
- Financing
- Making an offer, and
- Reading contracts

This list does not include all of the decorating, home improvement, and other decisions you will have to make once you have purchased the home.

If you are a first time home buyer, you will be nervous about finding the right home, investing money on a down payment, and being approved for financing. Once you have found a home, it will usually take between one or two months before you will be able to move in. In the meantime, you should plan the following:

- Moving arrangements
- Home inspections
- Yard sales
- Budgeting for paint and other supplies
- Taking time off from work, and
- Finding a lawyer if necessary

Proper planning will help you transition into your new home much easier than if you wait until the last minute to deal with these details. If you are planning on moving yourself, you should find a few friends or family members that will be willing to help as soon as possible.

New Homes vs. Older Homes

Another decision you will have to make is whether to buy a new home or look for an older one. Most first time homebuyers usually buy an older home, but this should not deter you from visiting a few builders to see what they are charging for the size home you are looking for.

Older homes may cost less, but they can be riddled with problems. In this book, you will learn what to look for when viewing a home, what to include in your purchase offer, and what to expect from a home inspection. There are many older homes that will need only minor repairs.

Which Home to Choose?

After you have looked into all of your options, you will be wondering which home to choose. There are many ways to find the home that is right for you. When looking at homes, you should keep these criteria in mind:

- Size
- Price
- Neighborhood
- Mortgage payments
- Repairs, and
- Additional features

While this is a short list, throughout this book you will learn other ways to find your dream home. In the end, you will just know when you have found the right home.

Moving into your first home will be an experience you will never forget. You should be excited as this is a little piece of the world that is just yours. Whether this is the home you will live in for a long time or just for a short time, buying a home will give you a sense of pride and of purpose. Not only will you have a mortgage to pay, you will also be responsible for making the home your own. When thinking about purchasing a home, you should begin saving your money for closing costs, repairs, and decorating materials.

One of the more rewarding moments will be when you get the keys to your new home and you begin making it your own with a little paint, furniture, and personal style.

Chapter 1 - Location, Location, Location

Choosing where to live is almost as important as the type of home you want to live in. While this is a very personal decision, there are pros and cons to every neighborhood. But wherever you want to live, you will have to know where the highways are located, grocery stores, schools, and how far from work you will be. Buying a home means more than the structure you will be living in. It is also the community and the accessibility to places and events that mean the most to you and to your family.

Finding the Right Neighborhood

How will you know you have found the right neighborhood? There are many ways to tell:

- You may feel a sense of calm
- The neighborhood may remind you of a happy memory
- You will be close to places you frequent often
- The neighborhood aesthetics are pleasing, or
- The rest of your family is pleased

You may feel one emotion or five when you turn the corner onto the street where you want to live. This will be an exciting time, especially if you have been searching for a home for the past few months.

When looking for the right location, you should consider the following:

- How clean is this neighborhood?
- Is this a high crime area?
- What is the average home value in the neighborhood?
- Are there community bylaws?
- What is the home close to?
- Is there garbage pickup?

While these questions may not include everything you are looking for when buying a home, they should be considered carefully as they will affect your life once you move into the home.

How Clean Is This Neighborhood?

You should look at the neighborhood at different times during the day to see how those who live in the neighborhood take care of it. If there is a lot of trash on the ground, the yards are not kept up properly, or there are old signs posted on trees and telephone poles, then the neighborhood may not be for you.

If the neighborhood looks clean and you see people outside caring for their lawns, then you may have found a community of people who care about where they live. This is an important factor if you are planning on living in the neighborhood for many years. All too often people will buy homes only to discover that they live in a neighborhood where people do not have respect for their property or the property of others. This can make selling the home much more difficult in the future.

Is This A High Crime Area?

While all neighborhoods will experience some crime, you should consider buying a home in an area that has a high crime rate very carefully. While the home itself may be the right price for your budget, it may not be located in an area that is right for your well-being.

Drive by the neighborhood at nighttime to see if there is adequate street lighting, suspicious activity, or anything else that might cause you to use caution. Research the neighborhood and find out how the crime rate compares to other neighborhoods. If the crime rate is too high, then it may be best to look somewhere else.

What Is The Average Home Value In The Neighborhood?

You can find this information out very easily by asking your real estate agent or by looking up this information at the county clerk's office or on their web site. You should be aware of the home values that are in your neighborhood for several reasons:

- Housing prices will vary depending on the neighborhood and region. You want to buy a home that you will be able to make a profit on when you decide to sell.
- You do not want to pay too much for a home.

- Giving a solid offer for the home means knowing what other homes that are similar in size are selling for.

Are There Community Bylaws or HOAs?

If you are looking at a home that is inside a community or home owners association, you should be aware of yearly dues, rules about what can be in your yard (pool, lawn decorations, etc.), and any other rules that they may have.

Many people enjoy living in an HOA community because they feel safe and want to meet others in the neighborhood. HOAs usually have picnics and other events during the year where neighbors can meet each other. Some communities have pools, tennis courts, and other amenities. Traditionally here in the Minneapolis / St. Paul Metro you will find these to be townhouses or condominiums. The Minneapolis / St. Paul Metro has very few HOAs that encompass single family homes.

What Is The Home Close To?

When choosing a home, you will need to find the nearest grocery store, schools, route to work, and other necessities that will make living in the neighborhood more convenient. Drive around the neighborhood to see what is around it. This will help make your decision to buy a home in a particular neighborhood much easier.

Is There Garbage Pickup?

While this may not seem like something you are interested in, when it comes to disposing of your trash, you may need to haul it to the dump yourself. Ask about trash pickup so that you can decide if this is something you really want to do on the weekend. This really is a question of living within the city limits or living in the country.

City Life vs. Country Living

Choosing the neighborhood you want to live in will also include deciding whether you want to live in the city, country, or suburbs. Many people with families usually want to live in the suburbs because there is more rooms for children to grow, but is still close enough for parents to commute to work.

But there are advantages to city and country living as well. Those who live in the city will be close to work, close to restaurants, activities, and events. Those who live in the country may have a longer commute to work, but they will be able to enjoy the peace and quiet of having fewer people around them. With communities such as Elk River, Jordan, Waconia and a large number of country acreage properties, there really are a number of choices for this topic that other areas may not have.

Whichever lifestyle you prefer, you should construct a pros and cons list that will give you a better idea of what to expect when looking for a home. Once you have looked at your list, you will have a better idea of which to choose. The following will get you started:

City Life

Pros

- Easy access to cultural events
- More options when eating out
- More grocery store and clothing store options
- Public transportation
- More people
- Choice of home styles, such as houses, condos, apartments, and
- Private and public schools

Cons

- Crime rates higher
- Pollution
- More people
- Higher housing costs
- Higher taxes
- Higher cost of living, and
- Not as much housing is available

County Living

Pros

- More land available
- New homes available
- Less people, and
- Cost of living is lower

Cons

- Fewer schools to choose from
- Further from grocery stores and other stores
- Less people
- Not as many cultural events, and
- Longer commute to work

Suburban Living

Pros

- Close to city and country
- More land
- Cost of living less is expensive than city living
- Close to cultural events, and
- Community feeling

Cons

- More people in a smaller area
- Fewer schools to choose from, and
- Long commute to work

When choosing the type of environment you would like to live in, the following may play a role in your final decision:

- Finances
- Schools
- Size of home desired
- Amount of land desired
- Taxes, and
- Length of your commute to work

You should check out both city and country living. While there will always be pros and cons, you should be able to find a home that will help you lead the type of lifestyle that is important to you and your family.

Making the Commute

You will have to count on the amount of traveling you will have to endure to and from your job when buying your first home. Unless you are relocating, you will have to find a neighborhood that is close enough to drive to or is accessible by public transportation. While some people enjoy sitting on a bus for an hour during the day, you may not want to use your time this way. Unfortunately, living in the suburbs or in the country may require you to make a longer commute.

If you want to remain relatively close to your job, you should not search further than a ten mile radius. Inform your real estate agent or drive ten miles in any direction and see what is out there. Many times there will be neighborhoods you have never even heard of. You should find back roads as well as highway accessible roads that will make your commute easier.

You should also look for a home during different times of day in order to figure out the traffic patterns. If possible, live in an area that goes against normal traffic patterns. That way you will not be stuck in traffic going to work or when coming home.

Commuting to work can easily turn into forty minutes, fifty minutes, or even an hour long drive depending on the time of day. While this may be inevitable, you should consider all of your options before purchasing a home.

Schools in the Area

If you have school age children, then you will want to find a home that is close to schools in the area. This goes for both public and private schools. If you find a neighborhood that you like, find out which school district it is located in. Not all districts are alike and you will have to send your children to the school district your home is located in.

While your children do not have to walk to school, being relatively close to home will make it easier to pick them up, participate in after school events, and give them a sense of community.

If you are planning on living in the country, the nearest school could be very close to home or very far away depending on where you move. The bus ride to and from school can be an hour or more. This could take time away from getting homework done or playing with friends. Be sure to weigh all of your options when choosing a home if you have children. Also, find out where the middle school and high schools are in the area. Eventually, your children will be attending these schools. Be prepared and find out everything you can about these schools as well.

Grocery Shopping and Other Necessities

While living in the country may seem peaceful, be prepared to do a lot more driving. The nearest grocery store or pharmacy may be thirty minutes or more. This is another factor you will have to consider when buying your first home. While small towns have centralized areas where the shops and grocery stores are located, unless you live in town, you will have to drive in order to get there.

Many people that live in the country will adjust their lives as well as their priorities. They may go to the grocery stores once every two weeks; they will not eat at restaurants as often, and will not go to the movies or other social events as often either. You will have to decide what is important to you.

Before buying a home, survey the town to see what is available. This will give you a good idea of what it would be like to live in an area. Spend a few days there if possible. This will save you from making a huge mistake later on.

If you are planning to stay in the city, you will have the advantages of public transportation, but you may still need a car for larger grocery shops. While the city can be convenient in many ways, parking a car is not one of them. You will have to pay for garage parking in many instances, which will end up costing you more money than if you lived in the country. But, you will be able to get to these stores quickly and easily at any time during the day.

Other Location Considerations

Other location considerations include:

- Weather
- Road conditions
- Location of property in the neighborhood, and
- Room to grow

You should be thinking ahead in terms of the weather. If you are planning on living in the country, for example, you should pay attention to possible flooding, snow, and other weather that could affect you getting to work. If the road is a dirt road, you should ask if the county will clear the road and how often they will do so. This is another advantage of living in the city because you could always use public transportation if you do not want to drive.

The location of the property is also important. If the property is located at the bottom of a slope, you may have flooding issues after a rainstorm. Also, as your family grows, you may need more room. You should find property that can hold a home addition if necessary. Investing in a home requires a great deal of thought and planning. Even if you do not have a family, you should find a home that will allow you to grow as your interests change.

Chapter 2 - Working With Real Estate Agents

If you are like many people, chances are good you looked around different neighborhoods, saw a few homes that were for sale, maybe visited an open house or two, and then felt stuck. What is the next step? Approach the homeowner? Visit a real estate agent?

Finding the right real estate agent when buying a home depends on what you are looking for in a home. You may have to visit several real estate agents before finding one that listens to your wants and needs. You should be comfortable working with them during the house hunting process.

Choosing a Real Estate Agent

There are a few ways to find a reliable real estate agent. For example, you can:

- Ask friends and family
- Ask other real estate agents
- Attend a few open houses and meet real estate agents
- Find ads online or in the newspaper
- Walk into a local office, or
- Look for local real estate agents in your neighborhood by paying attention to for sale signs in the neighborhood

- Ask me for my list of personally endorsed agents – these are agents that I have interviewed, screened, and meet my high standards and my personal seal of endorsement!

Asking plenty of questions before looking at houses may seem like a lot of work, but when you visit a real estate agent for the first time, you should think about questions that will help you get to know this person who is going to help you find your dream home. The five best questions to ask are:

1. Are you a certified real estate agent? How long have you been in the real estate business?
2. Which neighborhoods are you the most familiar with?
3. How many homes do you have that will fit my needs?
4. What is your typical commission on a home in my price range?

Once you have asked these questions, you should be looking for honest and complete answers, good communication, and eye contact. These are questions that the real estate agent should have practice in answering and should not have to give you a standard 'salesperson' answer.

If you feel uncomfortable, then you are under no obligation to continue with this real estate agent unless they have some good property matches to show you.

You should also pay attention to:

- How well your real estate agent listens to what you are looking for

- How well they understand current real estate law
- How many other clients they seem to have
- How they speak to their co workers
- How often they communicate with you on the phone or email

In the end, you will have to be the judge of the real estate agent. If they know what they are talking about, can find out the information you need quickly, and are willing to take the time to listen to what you need, then you should work very well with them.

In some cases, you may be asked to sign an agreement that states you will only be working with a specific real estate agency or agent when looking for a home. You are under no obligation to sign this paperwork and you should only do so if you feel very comfortable.

While these agreements are not totally binding, it could make buying a home more difficult down the road. Only sign agreements if you feel comfortable.

During your search for a real estate agent, you will find a variety of agents that will want to work with you. These include:

- Experienced agents
- New agents
- Pushy agents
- Absentee agents, and
- Hard working agents

While all real estate agents have different personalities, you will have to decide which ones you will want to work with when looking for your new home.

Experienced Agents vs. New Agents

This is an age old debate that should be addressed. While an experienced agent may have sold more homes and earned more commissions, new agents can be just as helpful and need to get some sales under their belt, which may prompt them to work harder for you.

While you should ask about their experience, you should take into consideration other traits such as the ability to listen and the ability to only show you homes in your price range. Experienced agents and new agents have been trained in a similar fashion and only have their personalities to bring to the table.

There are experienced agents out there who will drag their feet because they are over confident or they are not as interested in their jobs as they once were. Experienced agents may know more about different neighborhoods, but some of them are not as proactive as they used to be.

You should not let inexperience deter you when looking for an agent. Many times new agents will work harder because they want to gain a reputation that they can use to build confidence in their future clients

Pushy Agents

Unfortunately, you will meet real estate agents that will want to sell you more home than you need. In an effort to earn larger commissions or to sell those properties that are more difficult, many agents will try this tactic. This is where you will need to stand firm. You do not want to waste your time looking at homes that are beyond your price range unless you can find a way to lower the price.

While looking at possible homes is exciting, this will not last long as you will grow weary of spending all of your available time looking for a home. If an agent keeps showing you homes that are out of your price range, then you should consider finding another agent.

Absentee Agents

Absentee real estate agents are those agents who show you a few homes and then disappear for a few weeks. These agents may be overworked, may not be able to find a home in your price range or neighborhood, or have higher priced commissions to find. Whatever the reasons, this is unprofessional behavior and should be rectified immediately, especially if you need to find a home quickly.

If an agent does not have homes in your price range or neighborhood, they should recommend another agent in the group. Agencies never want to lose customers. If your agent does not do this, find a new one.

Even agents that are overworked have time to make a quick phone call. If you do not hear from your agent in a week after your last meeting, find another agent.

Hard Working Agents

These are the best agents to find when you are buying your first home. If you find an agent like this one, do not lose them. These are the agents that will follow every lead, pass your wants and needs to another agent, and try their best to find you a home. You should expect to see a handful of homes when working with an agent like this one.

Now that you know more about what to look for in a real estate agent, you should feel a little more comfortable about working with one. They can be an invaluable source of information when you want to know more about homes, neighborhoods, and other questions about the communities you are looking at.

When looking at homes with your real estate agent, you should ask questions about the home, the neighborhood, the city or town, and any other questions you need to know in order to make an informed decision. Part of your real estate agents job is to research homes and neighborhoods so that they can answer questions that may come up.

Preparing To See Homes with Your Real Estate Agent-Create a List

Once you have found a real estate agent you are comfortable with, you will want to make the most of your time when house hunting. Giving your real estate agent a list of what you are looking for will help narrow the search and save everyone some time. Your list should include:

- Your price range
- Number of bedrooms you want
- Number of bathrooms
- Size of property
- Basement (finished or unfinished)
- If you want a porch, patio or balcony
- Central heat and air conditioning
- Garage
- Neighborhood, and
- Any other amenities you would like

Giving your real estate agent a list of your preferences will allow them to spend more time researching homes that fit the criteria. You should list these amenities from greatest to least important because no home is perfect and you will not get everything you want or need. Let your agent know that you are flexible, but that you really want to concentrate on certain items when looking for a home.

Viewing Homes

When looking at homes with your agent, be sure to ask any questions you may have. While these questions may seem small, they may be important to your happiness. Common questions people ask their agents are:

- How old is the home?
- How many owners has the home had?
- What kinds of renovations have been done to the home?
- How old is the plumbing?
- How low are the sellers willing to go?
- How old is the carpeting and flooring?
- How old are the windows?

While your agent may answer some of these questions before you ask them, you should ask any questions that may influence your decision to buy a home. If you do not want to put too much work into fixing up the home, you may want to buy a home that is thirty years old or less.

If your agent does not know all of the answers to your questions, they should be able to find out and will give you an answer within a day or two.

Taking Pictures

One of the best ways to remember the homes you have seen is to bring your camera and take pictures. Get permission from the agent first before taking pictures of another person's home.

Many times, after looking at a few houses, you will forget how big the kitchen in home number two was in comparison to home number five. Having pictures will give you a better idea of the square footage and how much room you will have to work with.

Narrowing Down Your Choices

After a few weeks of viewing homes that fit what you are looking for, you should be close to finding a home that you will want to make a bid on. If you have other homes you would like to see or you have changed your mind as to what you are looking for, you should tell your agent so that they can look for other homes.

Many times, if a person likes the neighborhood but not the home they were shown, they will want to see other homes in the neighborhood that are for sale. You should ask to see all of the homes available in a neighborhood that you like.

If you are still not finding a home that you like, you may need to change the neighborhoods you are looking at. While this can seem disappointing, your real estate agent will be happy to show you homes in different neighborhoods. Sometimes if you compare homes to one another, you will find redeeming qualities in a home you have already seen.

Once you have found a home that you like, you should make an offer. Contact your agent as soon as you can so that they can draw up the paperwork, contact the seller's agent, and make an offer before another person does. Make an offer as soon as you can in order to avoid a bidding war.

Bidding can be long and drawn out in some cases. If you do not have the time to wait out a bid or if you cannot bid any higher, then you may be looking for another home to purchase. While this can set you back, you should try to stay positive and find a home that is right for you.

Your agent should be there to guide you along during this time. Ask all the questions you have to before making an offer on a home.

Information Real Estate Agents Should Tell You

There is plenty of information that real estate agents can tell you about the homes you will be viewing. Things they should tell you include:

- The price of the home
- The age of the home
- Any renovations that have been done
- Any other Issues with the home
- Property taxes
- Community dues
- Schools
- Neighborhood crime rates, and
- The median age of those who live in the neighborhood

Usually, if a real estate agent does not have the information you request on hand, they will be able to look it up once they are back at their office. You should be able to find out all the information you need to know in order to make an informed decision about buying a home. Real Estate Agents are required by law to give you information concerning repairs, damage, and the history of a home. This includes any incidents that have occurred inside the home such as criminal activity, fire, and other events.

You can also do a little research of your own by using the Internet, which has become a wonderful tool to use when searching for a home. You can research past events that have taken place in the neighborhood, the home itself, or the town where you want to live. Knowing a little history may prompt you to look elsewhere or make an offer.

Other information real estate agents can tell you include:

- Home owner price reduction (your real estate agent will talk with the seller's real estate agent once you have made an offer or want to make an offer to see how low the owners will go to sell the home)
- Prices of other homes in the area that are comparable to the one you are looking into buying
- How quickly the owner wants or needs to sell their home
- How much you will have to pay in property taxes each year, on average
- Other taxes in the area

Your real estate agent is a person that should be well acquainted with the neighborhoods you are looking at when buying your first home. Don't be afraid to ask many questions.

Working with Seller's And Buyer's Agents

As a homebuyer, your real estate agent is considered the buyer's agent. While some people will forego hiring an agent at first when looking for a home in order to save money on commission costs, they will usually end up hiring an agent to:

- Handle negotiations with sellers
- Do paperwork, and
- Survey neighborhoods

It is in your best interest to hire an agent in order to make buying a home a much easier, and faster process.

Negotiations with Sellers

Most people who sell their homes are also working with an agent. This agent is known as a seller's agent. If you choose not to hire an agent, you will be dealing with a seller's agent who is looking out for the homeowner's interests, and not yours.

Sometimes, though, the seller's agent and the buyer's agent can be the same agent. This means that your agent is looking after the interests of everyone involved. This is a rare occurrence, and it is best to hire a real estate agent that can negotiate with other agents in order to get you the best deal on a home.

Negotiating with agents can take a week or more depending on how high you are willing to go and how low the owners are willing to go. This can become a complicated game once you introduce home inspectors. After an initial home inspection, if you feel there are repairs that should be made prior to the sale of the home, or if you want a price reduction because of the repairs you will have to make, you will have to negotiate with the owners to settle on a fair price. Without an agent, you will have to do all of this work yourself.

Paperwork

When buying a home, there is a lot of paperwork that must be completed before the closing. This paperwork can include:

- Offers
- Counteroffers
- Home inspection reports
- Home appraisal reports, and
- Fixture lists

Filing the paperwork is not difficult, but it can take some time. Working with an agent will save you time and money when creating and sending out various paperwork.

Survey Neighborhoods

Another advantage to hiring an agent is that you will not have to do as much legwork in the beginning. You may have a few neighborhoods in mind, but you will be able to leave it to your agent to find homes for sale and setting up appointments to see them.

This is another time saver especially if you have to work during the week. Taking time from your busy day to call other agents and homeowners to set up appointments will distract you from your other daily duties.

More Reasons to Hire a Real Estate Agent

There are several other reasons to hire a real estate agent. These include:

Peace of Mind

The bottom line is that as a buyer, a buyer's agent is the best resource when it comes to finding and making an offer on a home. While a seller's agent will be able to tell you the basics about a home, they are working for the homeowner. They will not try to get you the lowest price for the home. If you enjoy negotiating, then working with seller's agents might be for you. But if you are like most people, hiring an agent to work on your side will make the entire process more enjoyable and worthwhile in the end.

Wealth of Knowledge

Your agent will be very knowledgeable about negotiating the right price for your new home, they will be able to help you decide where you want to live, and they will be able to guide you in buying or walking away from any property you are not sure about. This is why it is so important to talk with your agent and ask as many questions as you can before buying a home.

Confidence

If you are having doubts about purchasing the home you have made an offer on, then you should tell your agent right away so that they can postpone the offer made and help you reexamine what it is you are looking for in a home. Many times the initial shock of being a homeowner can be overwhelming. Sometimes talking with your agent is enough to resolve your feelings. Other times, you may need to see a few more homes before making a decision. Your agent will be able to give you practical advice during this time.

Chapter 3 - Playing the Housing Market: Buying vs. Renting a Home

Now that you know more about finding a real estate agent, you should begin watching the housing market carefully in the weeks or months before buying your first home in order to get a feel for whether it is in your favor.

Watching the Housing Market

For the past year, the housing market has been favoring buyers. Soaring market values were short-lived as many people decided they just could not afford to live in certain areas because of the cost of housing. This has caused many sellers to lower their prices. While this sounds like good news for you, the housing market can be very fickle. Depending on where you want to live, you may end up having to pay a small fortune for the home of your dreams.

This is why watching the market, surveying neighborhoods, and finding a good agent will help you in your search.

While you should not become a slave to the housing market, you should keep the following in mind before buying your first home:

- The past market value of the home you are interested in buying
- How much house your budget can get you in different neighborhoods and towns

- Neighborhood value
- How much the home should increase over time, and
- Price reductions that may be available

Just because you buy a home for a great deal does not mean you will make a huge profit when it is time to sell it. The housing market will continue to change and since this is your first home, you may want to choose something you can pay off quickly and make a larger profit on in the future.

Also, remember that any improvements you make on the home will increase its overall value. Just don't spend too much money on improvements. Creating a home improvement budget and sticking with it will help you make those monthly mortgage payments and other payments that will be due.

One of the biggest mistakes that first time homeowners can make is buying a home for a lot less than they budgeted and then making improvements that will end up costing more money in the end. If you can find a great deal on a home, use that extra money as a cushion in case you lose your job or are too ill to work. Owning a home is a big responsibility. Knowing how the market is moving and spending your money wisely will help when you are creating a budget, applying for a mortgage, and deciding how much to put down on a home.

Making the Most of the Housing Market

While you should be watching the housing market, there are other areas of interest you should be watching also, such as:

- National interest rates for mortgages
- Building rates in your area
- Number of foreclosures in your area, and
- Stock market and gasoline prices

National Interest Rates for Mortgages

Even though the housing market may be going your way does not mean that the interest rates you could be paying are. In the times when the housing market has taken a slump, interest rates tend to rise in order to retain the natural balance within the economy.

The interest rate you receive will depend on many factors, including:

- Other loans
- Current credit score
- Credit history
- Number of credit cards
- Yearly income
- Owed debts
- Current interest rates
- Type of lender
- Time of year, and
- Adjustable and fixed rate mortgage

If you see housing prices dropping, you may opt to buy a larger home than you would have if the prices had been higher a year ago. While you will be saving money on that end, you may be paying more each month because of the interest rate you received.

Building Rates in Your Area

If you notice the housing market has also caused the building of new homes in your area to decrease, then you may have to enter into a bidding war in order to buy your first home. When new home construction goes down, this can mean one of several things:

- The area is no longer popular
- The interest in buying a new home has diminished
- People can no longer afford to purchase new homes
- People are opting for older homes that are less expensive to heat and keep cool during the year

While that housing slump may bring a reduction of housing prices, you should consider making a bid soon after finding the home of your dreams because bidding wars will only end up costing your more money.

Number of Foreclosures in Your Area

When looking for a home, you should consider looking at homes that are under foreclosure. This can be for many reasons, but usually banks that hold the titles want to unload these homes quickly so that they do not lose more money than necessary. Many times auctions will be held or the home will be advertised as a foreclosure in the newspaper or online.

You should check out these homes because you may find exactly what you are looking for in a home.

Stock Market and Gasoline Prices

Even if you do not play the stock market game or own a car, you should still pay attention to these areas because they are usually what will dictate housing prices and the cost to heat and cool the home.

When the stock market is doing well many people will spend their money more freely, which will give way to higher housing prices. But when gasoline prices go up so will the price to heat and cool a home, which may make homebuyers reconsider buying until the prices fall again.

This could be a good time to buy a home if you are willing to pay a little more each month in utility costs.

The impact society can have on the housing market can be huge, and it can also have lasting effects. A buyer's market is created when there are more homes available than buyers, while seller's market occurs when there are more people who want to purchase homes than there are for sale. These housing markets go back and forth due to issues mentioned above.

In The End

In the end, when you are ready to buy a home, you should make the decision based on what you can afford and how much money you can put down for your new home. Just because you find a home that has a huge price reduction and you are not comfortable financially, does not mean you must buy that home.

Buy a home when you are ready. Many times, people will buy a home because it is cheaper in the long run than paying rent each month. The downside to home ownership is that you have to make your mortgage payments on time each month. Very few lenders will give you more time to come up with the money. If you miss even one payment, your home could be foreclosed upon. You will have no place to live and your credit score will suffer severely.

If you can afford to make the move into your new home now, you should not wait too long before making an offer. The housing market can change quickly and with competition out there, you may end up losing more money if you don't make an offer after seeing a home that you like.

Buying vs. Renting (Pros/Cons)

Even though in the long run buying a home is more cost effective than renting a home because of the equity that will build over time, many people are just not comfortable carrying the weight of paying for a home on their shoulders. Also, those who have to travel often for work may not want the day to day upkeep that owning a home requires.

There are plenty of pros and cons when it comes to buying a home versus renting a home. Since you are thinking about buying your first home, you should consider these pros and cons for several reasons. First, if you are currently renting a home, you may want to invest in property that you can later sell. Second, you will be responsible for repairs and maintenance for the home instead of being able to call your landlord or maintenance crew. The third reason you should weigh the pros and cons is if you are planning to move in the next few years. Since the housing market is a buyer's market for now, you may have difficulty selling the home later on.

Buying a Home

Pros

- Investment property – value will hopefully only increase or remain the same
- Build equity that you can use later on
- You can improve upon your home any way you want
- You can decorate it to suit your needs
- No landlord or property management company
- Sense of stability
- Ability to live in a community, and
- You have something to sell later on

Cons

- You are responsible for all repair and maintenance costs
- Monthly payments for utilities and mortgage are more expensive
- Could take time to sell later on

Renting a Home

Pros

- You are not responsible for repairs and maintenance costs
- Free to leave once the lease has expired
- In many cases, utilities are paid by the landlord
- Many apartment buildings have some sort of security system
- Usually less expensive than paying a monthly mortgage
- Credit score is unaffected if rent cannot be paid on time

Cons

- Privacy issues
- May have to share washer and dryers
- Rent to be increased once lease expires
- Landlord may not fix items on time
- Cannot paint walls or add other features
- Deposit may be required
- May not allow pets
- Neighbors come and go

As you can see, there are many factors that you should consider when thinking about buying your first home.

But if you are ready financially and want to have your own space, you should find an agent and start looking. The average time that most people take to make an offer on a home once they start looking is two weeks. If you have not found a home within that time, you should either continue looking or rethink your decision. There is nothing wrong with waiting a few months until you are ready.

Rent to Own

Another option you may have is to buy the property you are currently renting or rent a property that also offers you the option to buy after a certain amount of time. This will give you a chance to see if you like living in the home and will give you time to get your finances in order.

Rent to own properties are usually older than other homes and have been rental properties for some time. This means that they may not be in great shape. If you are looking for a property that you don't mind repairing, then this option may be for you.

When looking at a rent to own property, you should ask the following questions:

- How old is the home?
- How many times has it been rented out?
- What is the mortgage payment on the home?
- What is the rent per month for the home?
- How long will I have to make my decision?

- What happens if I change my mind?
- What happens if the homeowner changes their mind?

You should still sign the proper contracts stating that you are interested in buying the home after the given time period. This will protect your rights and the rights of the current homeowner.

New Homes

When you think of your first home, you may be thinking of a brand new home. Since the housing market is favoring buyers at the moment, you may get a great deal from a builder that is developing a new housing community, or you may find a plot of land that is in an existing community. This can be a great alternative to buying an older home for many reasons:

- You will have a part in designing the home
- You will have new appliances and lighting fixtures
- You will have new carpeting and flooring
- You will be able to choose all of the fixtures, carpeting, and flooring
- You will be able to add a porch or a patio, and
- You will be able to place the home where you want it on your property

A new home can be very exciting, but it can also be a lot of extra work. The first step in buying a new home is to find property. You should visit builders and real estate agents who will file all of the necessary paperwork, permits, and other items needed to build on the property. This can take a few weeks, so be sure to plan accordingly.

The next step is to design the home. This is the fun part where you will get to personalize your home to suit your needs.

Once you have been approved for a mortgage, the property has passed all of the land inspections, and the home has been designed, construction will begin. Depending on the time of year, you will have to wait about three months before you can move into your new home.

After construction is complete, you should complete a walk-through of the home, check all of the fixtures, and have the home inspected before signing the final paperwork. Then the home is yours.

Many people hire a lawyer during the construction phase so that all of the paperwork has been filed and there are no problems during the walk through.

Buying a new home is just one more option you should consider when looking for your first home. Home construction can vary as there are a few ways to build a home, including pre-fab homes that will be built elsewhere and delivered to your property where they will be assembled. Look into all of your options before deciding on a home that is right for you and your budget.

Using the Housing Market to Your Advantage

By paying attention to current housing trends and keeping a watchful eye on the homes in your area, you will be able to make an offer on a home that will be accepted. While the market is continually changing, it is a useful tool for those who are on a budget, who want to find a home that is large enough to suit their needs, and will be worth more when it is time to sell it.

When watching the housing market, consider the following:

- The number of homes that are in your area
- The number of days the homes have been on the market
- The price of a new home compared to those that are being sold by homeowners
- The price of renting vs. buying
- The number of homes that are in your price range
- The highest price you can pay when buying a home
- Interest rates in comparison to housing prices, and
- The time of year

Springtime is a good time to buy a home for several reasons:

- More people want to sell
- It is easier to make appointments to view homes
- Prices are usually lower
- People are more willing to reduce their asking price
- Income tax returns can help with a buyer's budget

There will be plenty of people who could not sell their homes in the fall or winter months and who are trying to sell before the summertime. Homeowners that need to sell their homes before a certain time are more willing to reduce the price of their homes.

While you should consider looking at a home during any time of the year, you will find that many homes will be lower in the spring to attract buyers.

This is also the time when interest rates are re-evaluated and many lenders are willing to give loans to those whose credit is not the best. Take advantage of when interest rates are at their lowest even if it means accepting an adjustable rate mortgage. You will have the option of locking into a fixed rate at a later time.

While the housing market can change, the idea of selling one's home will not. Homeowners may choose to wait out the current housing market, but if they are eager to buy another home or move to a new place, their wait will be short-lived. Negotiate with homeowners until a fair price can be reached. This is the same practice during a seller's market as in a buyer's market. You may have to play the bidding game for a week or two, but in the end, it is the person who needs to make the transaction happen the most that will end up compromising the most.

Chapter 4 - Home Inspections

A home inspection will give you a chance to discover more about the home before you purchase it. In case there are serious problems with the foundation, mold issues, radon or underground leaks, you will be prepared to ask for repairs, a reduced price, or walk away from the property.

The Importance of Home Inspections

Finding a home does not mean that your investigative duties are over.

What about full home inspections? Are they worth it? In most cases, the answer is yes. Although you will have to pay for a home inspection, it may save you a lot of money in the long run.

A thorough home inspection will include checking the following:

- Electrical systems
- Heating and cooling systems
- Foundation
- Siding
- Structural elements
- Roof
- Insulation
- Doors and windows, and
- Plumbing

If you are buying a new or used home, it is best to have a home inspection. Once the inspection report comes back, you will get the opportunity to ask the homeowners for a price reduction, go ahead and buy the home anyway, or ask the homeowners to make the necessary repairs.

You will receive a varied reaction from homeowners. Many times, they will agree to lower the price a little or fix some of the repairs.

When drawing up an initial offer for the purchase of the home, you should include a statement that allows you to withdraw your bid if any repairs are not taken care of or the price is not lowered due to the findings by the home inspector. In our market, this is normally known as the inspection contingency. If the contract does not include this, then you can still withdraw from the bid, but you may owe the agent commission fees and you may lose your earnest money.

Having a home inspection will give you peace of mind when you are buying a home. Since you will be taking out a mortgage, it is important to know what you will be buying, and the amount of money you will have to invest after purchasing the home. A home inspection will also help you make your final decision whether to purchase the home or to keep looking for another.

How to Find a Home Inspector

There are a few places to turn to when looking for a home inspector:

- Your real estate agent
- References from friends and family
- The phone book, and
- Contractors

Ask around and see if you can get references of other homeowners that will give you a good report. Many home inspectors work freelance and only work certain days during the week. They are trained in home inspection and many are retired contractors, builders, electricians, and plumbers who know what they are looking for.

When you find a few home inspectors, give them a call and ask the following questions:

- How long have you been inspecting homes?
- How much do you charge per hour?
- What do you look for when inspecting a home?
- What types of reports should I expect?
- What days during the week are you available?
- Do you offer septic system inspections?
- What type of licensing do you have?

A thorough home inspection should take an inspector about three hours to complete. This will give you an idea of how much the inspection will cost.

Once you have asked these questions, find out if your lender has specific inspections that the home must pass before you will receive a home loan. If the inspector can complete these inspections along with the home inspection, then it is worth the time and the money to have the inspector complete all inspections on the same day.

The next step after choosing an inspector and finding out which inspections will be needed by your lender is to make sure the homeowners will be home for the inspection. Usually your agent will arrange a time for the inspector to perform the inspection.

It is up to you if you would like to be present for the inspection or not. Many times, the reports will be enough to give you a clear idea of what needs to be done. After the inspection is complete and the reports have been completed, it is up to the homeowners to either make the repairs necessary or lower their asking price.

If the repairs are minor and will not require too much money to repair, they will usually agree to make the repairs. If you would like to absorb the costs of the repairs, then you can offer to do so. You should receive this decision in writing so that there is no confusion during the final walk through before the closing. At the closing, you should have all of your paperwork, including the home inspection reports with you in case there is a discrepancy.

What to Expect From a Home Inspection

A home inspection can unearth many problems you did not notice during your visits to the home. Typical findings include:

- Crumbling foundation
- Structural damage to floors, walls, and ceilings
- Water damage inside and outside the walls
- Porch railings or posts in poor condition
- Heating and cooling systems need to be cleaned or do not work properly
- Roof needs repair
- Broken or leaking pipes
- Electrical wiring not functioning or broken
- Broken water fixtures or light fixtures
- Windows that do not open
- Uneven doorways
- Improper insulation
- Mold
- Water contamination
- Septic tank issues, or
- Hazardous chemicals

Most homes will only experience a few minor issues, but some older homes may have more problems than they are worth. The damage to the homes could cost you thousands of dollars if you are unaware of the damage prior to purchasing the home. While disclosure of some problems is mandatory, many homeowners do not even know that some of these problems exist until they try to sell their homes.

On the day of the inspection, you should expect to hear about some problems. You should be given a detailed report of the findings that will outline drastic problems and those that can be fixed easily.

Some lenders will not approve the home loan until the problems are fixed and another inspection is conducted.

Specific Places That Should Be Inspected

When interviewing home inspectors, make sure to ask whether the following areas are inspected:

- Chimney and fireplace
- Attic, basement and crawl space
- Furnace
- Swimming pools and,
- Smoke detectors and appliances

These are important areas that can be very costly to repair once you have purchased the home. Many homeowners are willing to replace a chimney cap or remove mold from the basement. You should make sure that these areas are inspected prior to the closing. You should also inspect these areas during the final walkthrough.

Chimney and Fireplace

Inspectors should be looking for:

- Missing, broken, or intact chimney caps
- Mortar between brick chimneys is intact
- Metal chimneys are not bent or contain holes and have all screws in place
- Creosote – this is buildup caused from wood burning fireplaces, and is flammable if not removed

Attic, Basement, and Crawl Spaces

Home inspectors should be on the lookout for the following:

- Mold
- Fire damage
- Insulation
- Damage from water, and
- Damage from animals and pests

Furnace

There is nothing worse than dealing with below freezing weather and not having hot water or heat in the home. The inspector will check for cracks and leaks on the furnace.

Swimming Pools

When looking at the swimming pool, the inspector should look at the following:

- Swimming pool plumbing, and
- Swimming pool shell

Smoke Detectors and Appliances

- Make sure they work
- No leaks
- Check for broken hoses or connections
- Broken door handles
- Inadequate wiring

How Homeowners Will React

How the homeowner will react to the results of the home inspection could determine whether you continue pursuing the home or whether you let it go and find another one.

Homeowners have their own agenda when it comes to selling their home. These include:

- Buying another home
- Moving to another state
- Using the money to pay for family medical emergencies
- Retirement, or
- Making money on an investment property

This means that there are varying degrees as to what they are willing to pay for and what they are not willing to pay for. If the homeowner is not in a rush to sell, then they may contest the findings and refuse to repair certain items. If they need to make as much money as possible, they may agree to lower the price a little or make repairs that cost the least on the list.

You will have to make some tough decisions at this point. If the repairs that will be needed on the home are required by your lender, you can:

- Try to find another lender
- Try to get the homeowners to pay for the repairs
- Pay for the repairs yourself, or
- Walk away from the home

Whichever decision you make, you will have to live with the consequences.

Homeowners know they are taking risks when selling older homes, but what about new homes? If your new home does not pass inspection, it is up to the builder to make the necessary repairs. You should make sure this is included in the contract before signing it.

If you are buying a home that homeowners have already moved out of, you may be able to get the repairs paid for without having to be too pushy. If the homeowners are paying another mortgage, they are eager to sell and may opt to pay for the repairs upfront or give you a price reduction. This will depend on the circumstances. There is always a certain amount of luck that goes into buying a home.

Ways a Home Inspection Can Lower the Final Price

Even though you will have to spend money upfront for a home inspection, you may save more money than you anticipated once the results come back. This is especially true for older homes or new homes that were not built using the right materials or according to safety codes.

There are a few ways you will be able to negotiate a lower price on the home before signing the final contracts.

- **Ask homeowners to make repairs**

    This is the best way to save money on your new home. While you will not see a reduction in the final price of the home, you will not have to make as many repairs down the road. Also, you will not have to worry about the repairs once you have moved into the home.

    While all homeowners are different, you should be aware that many do not want to make repairs unless the home absolutely cannot be sold in the condition it is in because it will endanger the new owners. Even minor repairs may pose a problem for homeowners. You should be firm, but friendly when negotiating this part of the contract. If you do not want to make these repairs and you strongly feel that the repairs should be made by the homeowner, you can still walk away from the home and find another.

You should give homeowners a week to think about making the repairs. Most homeowners will make their decision quickly because they want the sale to go through.

- **Ask homeowners for a price reduction**

    If the homeowners do not want to spend money on the repairs that you have requested, they may agree to drop the final price of the home. While the price reduction will not be too drastic, any reduction is a good one since you will have to make the repairs yourself down the road.

    If the homeowners suggest a reduction in the final price, you should consider the offer and find out how much the repairs will cost you. If it seems like a fair deal, then take it. If not, you can always ask for a larger reduction. Most buyers and sellers eventually agree on a price that will suit both parties.

- **Ask homeowners to pay for all closing costs**

    Another way to save money without relying on the homeowners to pay for the repairs is if they agree to pay the closing costs on both sides. This will free up some of your money so that you can make the repairs yourself.

    You may have to have a separate contract drawn up that will explain what the homeowners are responsible for paying, and what you are responsible for paying. This will make buying the home much easier.

Any agreements that you make with the homeowners should be made in writing. Verbal agreements do not stand up in court, and are not common practice among real estate lawyers and agents when they are closing a deal. Your agent should make this clear to you at the beginning of the home buying process.

Do not be discouraged if there seems to be a lot of paperwork. This is necessary and the usual standard practice for those who want to protect themselves from wrong doing and lawsuits later on.

The Final Walkthrough

On the day of the closing, you should have a final walkthrough whether you are purchasing a new home or an older home. Final walkthroughs are a way for you to determine if there is anything else you will need to discuss, get in writing, or have changed before you sign the paperwork.

The final walkthrough will include you, the homeowners, real estate agents, and if necessary, your lawyer. Unfortunately, many buyers skip the final walkthrough in anticipation of moving into the home quickly. But you should have one more walkthrough just to be sure.

The benefits of a final walkthrough include:

- Making sure all repairs that were conceded by the homeowners have been made

- Be sure additional repairs are not necessary
- Walls are intact
- Plumbing is intact
- Flush toilets in the home
- Garage door opener
- Test doors and windows
- All appliances that were remaining are still in the home
- Appliances are in good working condition
- Electrical systems are working by turning on all lights
- All junk is removed from the yard as per prior agreements

You will feel much better after the final walkthrough for many reasons. You will get to see first-hand the repairs that have been made, you will begin to see yourself living in the home, and you will be able to plan for the future in terms of what you want to keep in the home and what you want to remove.

In some cases, you will never meet the homeowners. If they have moved before putting the house on the market, you may be dealing directly with the homeowner's lawyer or agent. It is still a good idea to ask questions about the home before signing the final paperwork.

The Closing

The closing is your last chance to ask for changes to the contract, to bring up any concerns, and to ask the homeowners any questions you may have about the home and the property.

At the closing, you should bring:

- A notepad
- Financial notes and mortgage approval paperwork
- Signed paperwork you have received over the course of the deal
- Identification, and
- The home inspection report

At this meeting, you will be signing the paperwork that will make the home yours. This is a very exciting time, but you should maintain your composure to make sure that you are getting what you are signing for. If repairs have not been made, then you have the option to wait until they are complete.

When to Walk Away

Any time after the home inspection if you begin to have doubts about purchasing the home, you should contact your real estate agent and voice your concerns. Many first time homebuyers need reassurance that they are making the right decisions. Your real estate agent will want the sale to go through, but they know that there are other properties they can show you, so they are not really losing money if you decide to not buy the home.

There are many reasons to walk away from a home sale. These include:

- A bad report from the home inspector

- The homeowners are unwilling to pay for necessary repairs
- You find another home that suits your needs
- The price for the home is too high
- You decide you don't like the neighborhood
- Loss of your job, or
- A medical emergency

Walking away from a home is not giving up on your dream of homeownership. Unfortunately, there are times in life when buying a home is not possible. If the financial strain is going to be too much, for example, then you should seriously consider finding a lower priced home or a smaller home.

If you decide to walk away from a home, you should give yourself a few weeks to recuperate before going out there and finding another home. You should contact:

- The real estate agent
- The lender, or
- The builder

Let them know of your decision and that you will be in touch when the time is right. Many times after a bad report from a home inspector, it is just not worth spending the money on a home that will require a lot of repairs down the road. While all older homes will have some repairs, you should know the limits of what is acceptable and what will cost you too much money.

If you can get enough financing and you want to pursue the home regardless of the repairs that will have to be made, then go for it. Sometimes buying an older home and fixing it up can be a fun activity for everyone involved. Only you can make these crucial decisions. A home inspection will help you realize how much work and money may be involved if you decide to purchase the home.

Chapter 5 - Financing Your First Home

Financing your first home can be the most frustrating part of the home buying process. This is the time when you will figure out how to pay for the home. Most people have to take out a mortgage loan in order to afford the price. Which mortgage loans are right for you? How much of a down payment will be necessary? What is escrow?

You will have many questions about financing your first home. By knowing the facts, paying attention to interest rates, and looking into all of your mortgage options, you will be able to choose repayment terms that will fit your current income and allow you to safely make those monthly payments.

Types of Home Loans

Deciding which home loan is the right one for you will depend on what you qualify for and what your lender is willing to give you. There are a few types of mortgage loans, including:

- Fixed rate mortgage loans
- Adjustable rate mortgage loans
- Balloon mortgages, and
- Jumbo loans

You should be familiar with these loans so that you will be able to make an informed decision when it comes to financing your new home.

Fixed Rate Mortgage Loans

For first time homebuyers who are on a strict budget, choosing a fixed rate mortgage may be the loan for you. Your monthly payment will never change for the life of the loan because you will lock into the interest rate given at the time the loan was processed. You can take out loans that range from ten to thirty years.

There are many advantages to taking out mortgage loans that have fixed rates. You will be able to create a monthly budget for yourself, you will never be surprised by the amount you will have to pay each month, and you will be able to lock into a low interest rate.

The disadvantages may not mean much to you now, but as your family or your income grows, you may want to refinance and pay less each month so that you will be able to afford renovations, vacations, and other luxuries. Since your mortgage is fixed, if interest rates drop, you will be trapped paying a higher rate. While you can refinance your mortgage, you will have to wait a certain amount of time, and even then there may be complications.

For those who have limited income, who have lower credit scores, or those who want the security of paying the same amount each month, then a fixed rate mortgage is the loan for you.

Adjustable Rate Mortgage Loans

If you expect to make more money in the next few years, and want to buy a bigger home, you may be interested in an adjustable rate mortgage. The major difference between an adjustable rate mortgage and a fixed rate mortgage is that the interest rate will vary year to year in an adjustable rate mortgage.

While the interest will be capped, you will still be paying more for each year that you own the home unless interest rates drop over an extended period of time. Most adjustable rate mortgages cannot be raised more than 2 interest points per year, and up to 6 points for the life of the loan.

These loans are good for those who want a larger home and who expect to increase their earning each year to afford the increase. If you are in a position to take out an adjustable rate mortgage, you will be able to lock into a lower fixed rate for 3, 5 or 7 years of a 30 year mortgage. The rate on this loan may be lower than a typical 30 year fixed mortgage. After the 3, 5 or 7 years of which you have chosen, then the loan would adjust on a yearly basis. The main advantage of these loans is that window upfront that you capture the lower rate.

Balloon Mortgages

If you are only planning on living in your first home for a few years (usually five to seven), you should look into a balloon mortgage. These mortgages require that you pay them off in five to seven years. They have a lower interest rate that is fixed.

If after the term of the mortgage has passed and you want to remain in the home, you will have to refinance and choose a fixed rate or adjustable mortgage to pay off the existing mortgage, as balloon mortgages cannot be renewed.

Only consider this mortgage if you are planning on moving after a certain amount of time or if you think you can pay the mortgage off in that amount of time.

At the time of writing this book, Balloon Mortgages are not an option with the new regulation. If you want a Balloon Mortgage, check with your Loan Officer if it is an option for you.

Jumbo Loans

Most first time homebuyers will not need to take out a jumbo loan unless they are buying a very large home. These loans are valued over $417,000 and are used to purchase land and a home. More collateral will be needed in order to qualify for one of these loans. The interest rates are comparable to fixed and adjustable rate mortgages, and have the same payment terms.

Now that you know about the types of mortgages that are available, you should be thinking about which lender to use. With so many lenders out there, it may be difficult to sort through all of them and find the right one. Doing a little homework will help you get the best deal possible.

Where to Find a Lender

These days there are many places to find a mortgage lender, such as:

- Internet advertisements
- Television advertisements
- Family or friends
- Your Current lender
- Your Current bank

As you can see, finding a lender should not be too difficult. You may have to contact several lenders before you find a lender that will give you a loan that meets your needs. When you apply for a home mortgage loan, the lender will check the following:

- Your credit score
- Your credit history
- Your current income
- Income of co-signer, in necessary
- References (professional and personal)
- Current interest rates based on the amount you are asking for
- Status of other loans you may have
- Number of years you have been eligible to work, and
- Number of years you have had credit

There are many factors that will go into your approval or denial of a home loan. You will have to be patient. You should contact a few lenders to see which ones will give you the best deal. Once the offers have been received, you will have to make some important decisions.

You should feel free to contact your lender at any time during the home buying process with questions and concerns you may have. Other important information the lender will need before granting you a loan include:

- The home inspection report
- Cleared title work, and
- The home appraisal

These reports are very important to a lender because they will tell the lender how much the home is actually worth and the types of damage that have lowered the overall value of the property. Lenders expect homeowners to remain in the home for at least five years. This will allow them to make a profit on the money they have loaned you. It is not worth it to them if you have to sell the home shortly after buying it because there is too much damage and you can no longer live there.

Applying For a Home Loan

When applying for a home loan, it is important to get the opinion of the underwriter. Most loan officers will take a look at your situation and give you their opinion based on their experience. It is the underwriter that gives the final opinion whether you are approved or not.

If you choose to work with a loan officer that can offer this option and you want to get pre-approved by an underwriter, you will have to bring the following information to the lenders office. It seems like a lot! It will make your life easier if you can get as much of these items together when the underwriter reviews the file.

- Most recent 1 month paystubs
- Federal tax returns (all pages) for the past 2 years
- W2 forms for the past 2 years
- If self-employed, provide all pages and schedules of past 2 years business tax returns and corporate K-1's
- Provide ALL pages of most recent 2 months statements for all accounts, including all checking, savings, stocks, IRA, 401k, etc. The statements must show your name, account number and the name of the banking institution.
- Copy of enlarged driver's license and social security card

You will be asked additional questions that will help lenders determine if you are able to pay the loan back on time. These questions include:

- Number of years renting a home or apartment
- Late payments on credit cards and other loans
- Active loans (such as student loans or car loans)
- Number of years at your current job
- Additional income

- Amount of the loan and number of years to pay it back
- Number of years living in an area
- Dependents that are living at your home

Applying for a loan can take a week or more. This is because background checks, credit checks, and references must be checked first before the loan will be underwritten.

In the meantime, you should be concentrating on gathering your paperwork, and sorting through your papers in case you cannot find everything the lender requests.

If you do not have your back tax returns, you can contact the IRS and request them by year. Many times, lenders will need to see returns from at least two years ago. Bank statements and bill statements from the past 2 months should be enough to secure a loan.

If you are turned down for a home loan, you will be notified as to the reasons why. This can be devastating, but you should develop a plan with the lender to determine a good timeline as to when you can buy and what is needed to buy. If your lender has not given you this plan, seek the advice of another lender and try to apply again. If you have poor credit, you may need to go through a lender that specializes in granting loans to those with poor credit. You may have to pay a higher interest rate, but at least you will be granted a loan.

Reasons for possible denial include:

- Poor credit or not enough credit
- Length of time at your job is too short
- Income level for the amount of loan requested
- Loan default
- Failure to pay rent or other bills, or
- Too much credit

Applying for a home loan can be stressful, but if you have good credit, steady employment, and enough income, you should have little trouble qualifying for a loan.

What Not To Do When Applying For a Home Loan

There are a few things you should not do after applying for a home loan:

- Buy a new car
- Begin a new job
- Buy new furniture and other large items using your credit cards
- Apply for a credit card, or
- Default on student loans or other loans

All of these actions will cause your credit score to change that will give lenders an inaccurate view of your spending habits and your overall credit score. If you take a job that pays less than you noted on your home loan application, your lender may not agree to grant you the loan.

If possible, do not begin a new job until you have moved into your home. Try not to spend money on credit cards. Buy furniture and other items using cash, or wait until you have signed the final contract and are a homeowner.

How Much Can I Afford

While there are many items that will change this number, the most important answer is do you have a budget? Most first time buyers have never put together a real budget. Use the following two forms to answer this question of what can you REALLY afford. The short answer lenders look for is what is called Debt to Income ratio or DTI. The second form will show you what your DTI will allow. In general your total DTI should not exceed 43% of your gross income. While that statement might seem scary and technical, the following forms will make this a very simple math problem.

BUDGET

Borrower Name: _____

Co-Borrower Name: _____

Address: _____

City, State, Zip: _____

INCOME SOURCE	INCOME
Borrower Gross Income	
Co-Borrower Gross Income	
TOTAL GROSS INCOME	
TOTAL NET INCOME	

EXPENSE DESCRIPTION	AMOUNT
Rent	
Food	
Utilities (gas, water, electric, trash)	
Gasoline	
Cell Phone & Land Line	
Home Maintenance	
Dry Cleaning	
Housekeeper	
Child Care	
Visa, MasterCard, Dept Store payments	
Car Payment	
TOTAL EXPENSES	

TOTAL NET INCOME	
TOTAL EXPENSES	
EQUALS ABILTY TO SAVE	

Increase Your Chances for Approval

There are a few ways to increase your chances for loan approval that will also help you determine what you will be able to afford each month:

- *Pre-approval*

    Many experts agree that applying for a loan **before you find a home and being pre-approved** will help you create a budget, buy a home that is in your price range, and help lenders make their decisions faster.

- *Ask for only the amount you will need*

    One way to increase your chances for a home loan is to not ask for more than you will qualify for. This means you will have to look at your income level, the amount of debt you have, and the expected monthly mortgage payment. You should also factor in cost of living expenses, because your lender will. Apply for the amount you will need and nothing more.

- *Pay off credit cards*

    If you are thinking about buying a home in the next few years, you should prepare by paying off those credit cards and only using them for emergencies. Do not cancel your existing cards since this may actually lower your credit score. By showing you have a zero balance on your credit cards, you will be showing lenders that you know how to use credit wisely and you have been paying your cards off on time.

- *Always pay bills on time*

    This includes your electric bill, rent, student loans, and other bills that you may have to pay each month. By creating a track record that can be traced, you will be showing lenders that you are a responsible person who deserves to have a home loan.

What makes up my credit score

Credit scores and the formulas that the three major credit bureaus use are a closely guarded secret. However, in general here are the five major areas that the agencies look towards when determining your score.

- Payment history
- Amount owed on current accounts
- Length of credit history
- New credit
- Credit mix

How Home Appraisals Can Affect Your Home Loan

Unfortunately, a home appraisal can affect the status of your loan. If the home appraisal comes under the selling price of the home, most lenders will not grant the loan. This can be heartbreaking, but there are a few solutions that may work depending on the rules of the lender. The following options are available:

The Homeowner Reduces the Selling Price

Depending on the appraised value in comparison to the asking price, some homeowners will be willing to lower the price of the home if they need to sell quickly.

You should not count on this happening since many homeowners want to receive the price they are asking for. You may have no choice but to find another home.

A Higher Down Payment

Some lenders will grant you the loan if you agree to pay a larger down payment on the home and assume the financial risk. This is only an option if you can afford to pay a larger down payment.

Dispute the Appraisal

You can send a letter to your lender disputing the appraisal or have another appraiser determine the value of the home. You will have to pay for this second appraisal, which may or may not yield the same results. There is no guarantee that your lender will accept the second appraisal.

The Mortgage Timeline

Most mortgages can be closed in 21 days. In today's market it is not uncommon to run into delays with lenders that might take up to 60 days to close your loan. Below is a general guide of the traditional timeline, but be sure to ask your lender what they expect the closing to be. Again some lenders can close loans in as little as 21 days while another lender across the street might take as much as 60 days for that same loan transaction.

- Step 1: File Submission – The lender gathers the required documents upfront to ensure a good submission to an underwriter. The more you get upfront, the easier the process becomes. (1-2 days)
- Step 2: Upfront Underwriting – Underwriter reviews the file – (1-3 days)
- Step 3: You find a property – (1-2 weeks)
- Step 4: The lender is required to disclose the file to you – This could be as many as 60 disclosures!
- Step 5: The lender orders title and appraisal – Appraisals can take up to 2 weeks.
- Step 6: Any outstanding conditions the underwriter requested in the initial underwriting is submitted back to the underwriter for the final review (1-3 days)
- Step 7: Closing documents are sent to the title company

When you are choosing a lender, make sure you interview them on the process to see how organized they are. As you can see from the steps, this can be a lot of work. A good organized lender can help streamline the process, making it easier for you to navigate through this process. Also, the more you can get to the lender upfront can save you time during the process too.

Additional Fees for Home Loans

You may notice that you will have to pay small fees throughout your home buying experience. It seems that every piece of paper you sign, file, or request will cost you some money. Here is a list of fees that you may be charged:

- Credit report fee
- Loan discount fee
- Appraisal fee
- Loan origination fee
- Mortgage insurance application fee
- Hazard insurance
- Title search, and
- Title insurance

These fees can add up, so you will want to be prepared and have a little extra in savings for when these fees come up. Some of these fees can be put off until the closing, but you should be planning for them in advance.

Loan Estimates

Many lenders have turned to loan estimates that are supposed to help you afford your new home. Many of the above mentioned fees may be added up and paid at the closing.

When looking for a lender, you should compare estimates to see which lender is the lowest, which are the highest, and which are in the middle. All too often these estimates are too low. Some lenders will do this on purpose in order to get you to take out the loan. By comparing estimates, you will be able to get a better idea of which lenders are honest and which is not.

As a rule, you should expect to pay between three and five percent of your loan in closing costs. A loan estimate will give you an idea of the final cost, but you should keep track of what everything costs and try to have extra money set aside just in case.

Escrow and Other Loan Terms

As you are going through the home loan process, you will run across a few terms that you will not understand. You should ask your lender to explain these terms so that you will fully understand the type of loan you are applying for, the lenders policies, and other information that will be important throughout the life of the loan. Here are some common terms you may encounter:

- ***Escrow***

    While this term can mean different things in different situations, you will see it often when closing on a home. Your lender will set up an escrow account at close to insure Taxes are paid in May and October and that your insurance is paid once per year. Depending on what month of the year you close will determine how much money is put into escrow. The lender can't have more than 2 months as a buffer.

- *Mortgage*

    Even though you have heard of a mortgage before, you probably thought of it as the home loan you will be paying once you move into your new home. Technically, a mortgage is a lien on your home created by your lender. If you cannot make payments on your home, the lender will have the right to sell the property in order to gain the money that they have lost.

- *Foreclosure*

    This is a term that refers to homes whose owners could not make payments each month. Once a lender has decided to sell the home, it will be in foreclosure. You should find out ways to work with your lender in case you miss a mortgage payment at any time. Having this knowledge in advance will make financial emergencies easier to deal with.

- *Points*

    Some lenders refer to points as discount points and some lenders refer to points as origination. If you are shopping loans, make sure you are taking into consideration all the lender fees. In the end it is about comparing what your monthly payment is and how much you have to bring in to the closing.

- ***Down Payment***

    A down payment is helpful in several ways. It will lower the amount of money you will need for a home loan, it will allow lenders to see that you are responsible for paying off a mortgage, and it will move the home buying process faster. It will save you money by putting 20% down, but most first time homeowners will put no more than 5% down for a down payment. You do not want to overextend yourself by putting a huge down payment on a home because you may not have enough money to pay your mortgage, afford new furniture, or make home repairs.

- ***Debt to Income Ratio***

    This is one way that lenders will look to determine if you can afford your monthly mortgage payments on your current income. The lender will subtract all your reoccurring debt to determine how much is left for a mortgage payment.

    This is why not buying a car or spending money on your credit cards is so important when buying a home. The less debt you have will mean more available money for your mortgage payment.

- *Private Mortgage Insurance*

    If you cannot afford to put down more than 5% on a home, you may not be approved for a loan. But if you purchase private mortgage insurance, your lender may agree to give you the loan. This extra insurance will protect the lender in case you default on the loan by paying them at least 15% of the total loan value. This will cost you a little extra each month, but it may be worth it.

- *Credit Report*

    Before you apply for a home loan, you should obtain copies of your credit report so that you can check for errors; see how much money you owe on credit cards and loans, and to see what your credit score is. This is another way that lenders will determine if you will receive a loan.

    There are three credit reports that you should obtain, because you will not know which one the lender will base their decisions on. While the numbers from these credit reports should not vary too much, if you see any major discrepancies, you should contact the agency and have the mistake corrected. You are entitled to one free credit report per year by contacting the IRS for more information.

Chapter 6 - Making a Realistic Offer

By this point, you should have found a real estate agent, contacted a few lenders, and seen a few homes. If you have not made up your mind on a home yet, you should take your time and keep looking. But keep in mind that if you wait too long, you may end up in a bidding war with another buyer.

Making an offer on a home is a huge step. You will be taking on the responsibility of a mortgage, repairs, lawn care, and other chores that homeowners sometimes gripe too much about. While you should be cautious, you should also make a bid on a home that you really like within a week after seeing it. This will put your mind at ease so that you can think of all the other items you will have to get done before the closing.

What to Do Before Making an Offer

Before you make an offer on a home, you should do the following:

- Attend open houses
- Find out more about a property, and
- Find out about taxes in the area

These suggestions will help you make the most informed decision possible when it comes to buying your first home.

Attend Open Houses

Attend as many open houses as you can in homes that are in the area where you want to live. This will give you the opportunity to see; what is out there, the going price of homes in the area, and also give you a basis of comparison when looking at other homes.

Open houses are fun because you will be able to look into every area of the home without having to worry about the homeowners and real estate agents following you around. Many times, you may even find your new home this way.

Almost every weekend in most neighborhoods, there will be an open house. Stop by and see for yourself what the homes in the area look like and what you can get for your budget.

Find Out More about a Property

If you find a home that you might want to buy, you should find out everything you can about the property first before making an offer. If you go to the county website, you can see what the tax estimated value, how much the taxes are and sometimes you can see how much the previous owner paid for the home. This will give you an idea of how much you should offer for the home. If the home is in an area that has seen better days, then you can make an offer that is less because when you sell the property someday, you may have to lower your price as well.

Find Out More about Taxes in the Area

As a homeowner, you will be paying yearly property taxes, local taxes, school taxes, community dues, and other taxes that could drive your household spending through the roof. Before you commit to living in a certain area, make sure you understand everything you will be paying each year.

Your real estate agent should have the neighborhood information that will help you decide where you want to move. You can also visit your local tax office and see how much the current homeowners paid in taxes last year.

When you visit a lender, you will have to figure in your taxes as household expenses. This will be deducted from you income, which will leave you with less each month to pay your mortgage. Just because you may have found a home that is within your budget, you may not be able to afford the taxes that come with it.

How to Write a Purchase Offer

This is the most important step when making an offer to buy your first home. The purchase offer should outline everything you expect from the homeowner and what they can expect from you. You should include the following in your offer:

- price being offered
- amount of deposit on the home
- amount of money you will be putting down on the home
- mortgage terms

- Contingencies (such as appliances that will stay repairs that will need to be made, removal of items in the yard, etc.)
- when closing will take place
- specify who will pay which fees
- any reports that will be needed, and

Each of these categories should be explained in its own paragraph. You should try to be as specific as possible when writing up a purchasing offer. Each state has its own laws concerning contingency, amount of time a buyer has to respond to the offer, and fees that are to be paid. Be aware of these laws before sending your offer or you may end up with a counter offer or a rejection.

Making an Offer

After completing your research, you will be ready to make an offer on your first home. You will have to visit your real estate agent to sign a formal agreement that will outline your offer and for how long you will be making this offer. Most agreements will give sellers three days to a week to consider the offer.

In this time, the offer may be accepted, rejected, or a counter offer will be made. You will have to decide what you will want to do next if the offer is rejected or another offer is made. If the offer is accepted, then you will have to contact your lender, a home inspector, and make arrangements for your move.

Most homes will go to closing within a month after an offer has been accepted. This may seem like a long time, but it is not. You will have plenty to do in the meantime.

Low or High Offers

Hopefully, by researching the neighborhood, the property, and the value of the home, you will be able to come as close to the sellers price as possible. Sometimes, though, this is not possible. There may be circumstances that may prohibit you from making an offer that is close to the selling price.

Low Offers

Low offers are usually the result of the selling price being too high, ignorance of the buyer, or the buyer not having enough money to pay that asking price. Whatever the reasons, you should be careful when giving a low offer to a homeowner.

If you have specific reasons for offering a lower price, they should be mentioned in the offer so that the homeowner has a better understanding of how you came to the price offered. In some cases, the seller may offer a counteroffer, which you can either accept or reject. But if the homeowner feels insulted by the lower offer, they may just reject the offer and move on to another.

High Offers

The only time you should make an offer that is higher than the asking price is if other offers have been made. While this could be the beginning of a bidding war, if you offer just a little more than the highest bid, you may win. You should only do this if the property is worth it and you will be living in it for a long time.

If you make an offer that is high, then you will not leave any room for negotiation. Depending on the homeowner's circumstances, they may have been willing to go a little lower in order to sell the home. But since you made an offer that was higher than the asking price, you will end up paying more than you should have.

Many times, first time home owners make the mistake of wanting a home so badly that they are willing to pay a few thousand more than the home is worth. This is money that could be used for a down payment.

Making the Right Offer

The closer you can come to the asking price, the better off you will be. Once the home inspection is complete, the homeowners may have to come down in price anyway because of the repairs they will have to make.

Making the right decisions when buying a home are not always made quickly. You should play by the rules and just see what happens. If you get into a bidding war and cannot bid any higher, then it is best to let the home go and find another. You should not be a slave to your first home by buying one that is over your budget. There are many homes available if you keep looking.

How to Handle a Counter Offer and Offer Rejection

Sometimes, if you give homeowners an offer that is lower than their asking price, they may offer a counter offer. This is usually an offer that is more than your offer, but a little less than the asking price.

Counter Offer

Depending on where you live, the laws pertaining to counter offers will vary. Typically, the number of counter offers is limitless, but no counter offer can be the same. While counter offers are usually concerning money, these offers may also contain the following:

- Ownership of appliances
- Repairs
- Time frames for closing, and
- Time frames for counter offers

Buyers and sellers may only have hours to accept, reject, or offer another counter offer after receiving one. This can be a very stressful process, especially if you are dealing with a seller that has other offers on the table. While most homeowners will reject an offer if it is too low or they have received another, some will try to get the most they can from the sale that can include the smallest items in the home.

If you are determined to buy a home, but still want a lower price after the buyer has reacted with a counter offer, you can try to find a price that will suit everyone's needs. If you are making a counter offer that does not make that much of a difference, you should weigh the odds that another offer has been made, the homeowner will reject your offer, and that time is ticking for everyone.

Try your best to accept the counter offer before making one of your own. Is it really worth losing your dream home over one or two thousand dollars?

Dealing with Rejection

The hardest part about an offer rejection is that the homeowner does not have to answer your offer. If you do not hear from the homeowner within a week, it is safe to assume they are not interested in your bid. While this can be frustrating, you will have to move on. Begin your house hunting again and try to stay positive.

If the homeowner gives you a response in the form of a rejection, they may site the reason why in the paperwork. If your offer was too low, they had another offer, decided not to sell, or want to wait for a higher offer, at least you can move on without wondering why your bid was rejected.

Considering Items in the Home

When you are writing your purchase offer, you should consider the items that you would like to keep and items you would like to have removed from the home. These items can include:

- Certain appliances (such as the washer and dryer)
- Lighting fixtures
- Storage fixtures
- Single air conditioning units that fit into windows
- Hardware from windows and doors, or
- Pools

You should put these items in writing so that you will get them with the home. Some homeowners may try taking certain items with them either because they didn't know that you wanted them or because they were not supposed to be sold with the home to begin with. Be sure to obtain a list of items the homeowner is selling with the home so that you can compare it to your list.

This can also work in reverse. If there are items that you would like removed from the home or the property before you move in, you should specify these in the offer. These items can include:

- Old patio furniture
- Mechanical equipment
- Old appliances, and
- Light fixtures

By putting all of these items in writing, you will be helping to move the buying process along. While the homeowners may not agree with everything that you may want to keep, it will be up to them if they want to continue the process. Having everything in writing will leave people with no surprises during the closing.

Understanding the Seller

One of the key elements of making a solid offer is having an understanding of the seller. Your real estate agent will be able to tell you a little about the seller that may help when trying to come up with a fair offer.

When deciding on an offer for the home, you should find out the following about the seller:

- How eager are they to sell their home?
- How long have they lived in the home?
- How many offers have they received?
- How many have they turned down?
- Have they lowered their asking price?
- Are they relocating to another area?
- Do they need to sell their home quickly?
- Are they waiting for their asking price?

These questions, although you may not know the answer to some of them, will help you make an offer that will be looked at by homeowners and taken seriously. Sometimes when a homeowner needs to leave the area in a certain amount of time they will lower their asking price. This could be an advantage for you, but if the homeowners have already lowered the price, they may not want to lower it any further.

Make a reasonable offer and see what happens. Depending on the circumstances, it may be accepted.

What To Do in a Buyer's Market

In a buyer's market, you will have more choices when it comes to the types of homes you can purchase. Depending on how long the market favors the buyer, you will also have the luxury of taking your time because bidding wars are much less. When buying your first home, you should check out all your options. That home you couldn't afford a few years ago may be in your price range today.

When looking for a home in a buyer's market, you should do the following:

- Stay current with the listings in your area
- Sign up for free email listings and newsletters
- Check out homes that have recently been reduced
- When making an offer, ask for closing fees to be paid for by the seller
- See if there are other offers, such as appliances that come with the home
- Ask for certain allowances (carpeting, roofing, siding, etc.)
- Do not be afraid to offer a lower price, and
- Ask for a shorter response time

In a buyer's market, homeowners may offer these options to you as incentive to buy their homes. They may also offer warranties on appliances that you should take advantage of.

There are dangers that you should consider when buying in a buyer's market, however.

- If you are not planning on living in the home for more than three years, you may want to wait until the market changes or plan to live in the home longer. Many times, market trends can last for a few years. If you need to move after a year or so, you may have difficulty finding a buyer and you may have to sell the home for less than what you paid for it.
- While most homeowners stay in their homes for at least two years in order to save money in taxes, marketing trends have been known to last longer. You should be prepared for this when buying your first home.
- Make sure a thorough home inspection has been completed before buying the home. If you decide you cannot live there after you have bought the property, you may have difficulty selling it and you will have to spend more money making repairs.

Even though you cannot predict how the market will change, you should consider a home that you can afford, that you will want to live in for a long time, and one that can be improved upon while you own it.

What To Do in a Seller's Market

In a seller's market, you will have to play the game slightly different than you would in a buyer's market. In this type of market, there are many buyers who will want to buy homes that are attractive and priced within their budget. Homeowners will have their pick of offers to choose from so your offer will have to stand out in more than just price.

When looking for a home in a seller's market, you should:

- Make an offer that is close to the asking price or slightly over
- Send a pre-qualification letter from your lender with the offer
- Choose a closing date that is sooner rather than later
- Do not ask for too many contingencies
- Send a personal letter
- Promise more of a down payment, and
- Use a real estate agent that gets things done quickly

In a seller's market, you may also want to think about the dangers of buying a home. If you make an offer that is too high and you find out later on that the mortgage payments will be a struggle, you may have to sell. Depending on changes in the market, this may be more difficult than when you were looking for a home.

Buying your first home during this time may also be difficult because you will not be able to put much down, you may only qualify for a certain amount of money which may not be enough to compete during a bidding war, and you may be out bid by those who have more experience than you do.

When you decide to buy a home, you should be looking at your finance situation, the market, and the asking price for the homes you are interested in making an offer on. If you can wait a few months to see where the market is headed, then maybe this is the best way to save more money and find a home that is affordable. This is a waiting game that no one wants to play, but may be necessary, especially if this is your first home purchase.

Seller's markets and buyer's markets have their advantages and disadvantages, but in the end, the offer that you make will determine whether your offer will be accepted.

Chapter 7 - Contracts, Home Warranties, and the Closing

Drawing up contracts, having the final walkthrough, and going to the closing are the last steps you will have to take when buying your first home. This is the time when having a real estate agent you can trust, and a little knowledge of home buying comes in handy.

Contracts

Your purchase offer was the first contract you will be involved in when you want to buy a home. You should refer to this contract during the closing period to make sure that your rights are covered and that you are getting everything you pay for.

By writing a solid purchase offer that outlines what you want from the homeowners, you will be protected in case of disagreements and other issues before closing. But a purchase offer is just one of many pieces of paper you will have to see and sign before you can move into your home. Other contracts include:

- Contingencies
- Builder contracts
- Mortgage contracts, and
- Closing agreements

These contracts may vary in length depending on the forms being used and the information that will have to be included.

Contingencies

Real estate contingencies can be added onto an existing contract or can be created as a separate contract depending on what you would like to include in the purchase offer. Contingencies can include a wide range of items, including:

- Home inspections
- Home appraisals
- Financing
- Septic system tests

Contingencies can make or break a sale, so you should be sure to use the correct forms when filing contingencies and to word them correctly.

You will need to include a resolution for repairs that may need to be done before you can move into the home. If it is agreed upon in writing that the homeowners will take care of all or some repairs that may be found during a home inspection, this will save time later on.

You should also include ways to get out of the deal that include loan denial, repairs that cannot be fixed, and lead, mold, or radon that is found in the home. Having a way out of the contract will save you money and time.

If you are buying a home that is for sale by owner, you should find a real estate agent that is willing to help you create a contingency list and edit it where necessary. Do not rely on the seller's agent because they are after their client's best interests and not yours.

Builder Contracts

If you are buying a new home from a builder, you will have to sign a builder's contract that states you have the financial means to pay for a new home, that you have decided on a location for your new home, and that you are ready to build.

You should hire a real estate agent at this point to go over the contract to see if there are any problems that will have to be ironed out before you begin building the home.

Mortgage Contracts

In order to complete your home buying, you will have to be approved for a mortgage by a lender and you will have to sign a contract in which you agree to an interest rate, monthly payment schedule, rate plan, down payment, and other fees.

These contracts are standard loan contracts that will explain the consequences of not paying your mortgage. You should read this paperwork carefully before signing anything.

Closing Agreements

These are the final contracts you will have to sign before you get the keys to your new home. You should read this paperwork carefully and be prepared to pay any closing costs at this time.

Home Warranties

If you are buying an older home, you may want to purchase a home warranty that will cover repairs that will have to be made during your first year of ownership.

While a home inspection will catch any immediate repairs, no one can foresee an oven falling apart or a dryer burning out. Since you may not have a lot of extra money left over after paying for closing costs, down payment, and mortgage payments, having extra insurance will allow you to make the repairs you will need.

Most policies will cost between three-hundred and five-hundred dollars. Coverage will begin the day of your closing and will last for a year. You will have the option of renewing the policy if you would like at that time. If you need to have an appliance repaired, you may have to pay small co-pay at the time of the repair.

Not all policies are the same, so you should do your research to find the best deal. Compare the types of repairs that are covered under the policies and choose the one that fits your home.

Closing

When you finally arrive at the closing, you should expect to:

- Sign contracts
- Do a final walkthrough
- Pay closing costs, and
- Get your keys

The closing can take up to an hour, but usually moves quickly because there is little left to do. At the closing you will probably meet the homeowners. This could be the first time you will meet them. This is a good time to ask if there is anything about the home you will need to know.

Sign Contracts

When you sign the contracts, read them carefully to make sure that everything that has been discussed is in the contract. Ask questions that you may have at this time.

Final Walk Through

The final walkthrough of the home will take place before the closing. This is the final chance for you to see the home before it becomes yours. Make sure the items on your contingency are in place so that you can sign the contracts. If you have a lot of items that need to be repaired, it might be good to do this walk through a week in advance. This will insure that the seller has done everything on your list. If they haven't, then the seller has time to finish and it won't delay your closing.

Paying Closing Costs

Typically in our Twin City market, you can add a contingency to have the seller pays most of the closing costs. In a seller's market, the buyer may have to pay more of the closing costs associated with buying a home. This may appeal to sellers who want to sell their home quickly.

Get Your Keys

After signing the contracts, you will receive the keys to your new home. This is an exciting feeling and one that will be with you for a long time.

Conclusion

When it comes to purchasing a home, you may find that it takes a long time. You might find the home you love on the first showing, but for most people in the Minneapolis / St. Paul Metro, it takes at least 10 home showings before you decide to buy. There are some real estate agents who will show you that many in a day! The amount of homes you see, is completely up to you and how good your real estate agent is.

If you can get pre-approved by a lender using an underwriter's opinion early in the process, it will help you determine a purchase price that will fit your budget.

The real estate agent will ask you some basic questions about price and features, and send you properties that fit your criteria. A good real estate agent will also look in the neighborhood you want to buy and suggest homes to look at too. When you find a home you want to look at, request a showing right away. A good home will sell fast.

This will be one of the biggest decisions of your life. Good planning with a lender up front and working with a great real estate agent can save you time, money and make the process go smoothly.

Made in the USA
Lexington, KY
29 October 2016